AFTER MONTALE

AFTER MONTALE

ROY MARSHALL

All rights reserved. No part of this work covered by the copyright herein may be reproduced or used in any means—graphic, electronic, or mechanical, including copying, recording, taping, or information storage and retrieval systems—without written permission of the publisher.

Printed by imprintdigital
Upton Pyne, Exeter
www.digital.imprint.co.uk

Typesetting and cover design by narrator
www.narrator.me.uk
info@narrator.me.uk
033 022 300 39

Published by Shoestring Press
19 Devonshire Avenue, Beeston, Nottingham, NG9 1BS
(0115) 925 1827
www.shoestringpress.co.uk

First published 2019
© Copyright: Roy Marshall
© Front cover photograph by Roy Marshall

The moral right of the author has been asserted.

ISBN 978-1-912524-40-2

"We are far more united and have far more
in common with each other than things that divide us."

– Jo Cox

CONTENTS

Preface	1
Don't Ask	3
Midday	4
Light	5
Sunflower	6
The Evidence	6
Syria	7
Portovenere	8
Frown	8
Smoke	9
Rain	9
Wind and Flags	10
Shoot Growing In a Wall	11
The Dead	12
The Wind on the Crescent	13
I'm Not Asking	13
Lemon Trees	14
Death Didn't Trouble You	16
The Shoehorn	17
You	17
Hawks	18
The Flood	19
Red on Red	20
The Kingfisher	21
The Big Deal	22
Remorse	22
History	23
Götterdämmerung	25
Acknowledgements	27
Selected Bibliography	27

PREFACE

Both Montale and my Italian grandfather were born in Northern Italy in the 1890's. Both were soldiers on the Austrian front in World War One. Both lost employment and faced challenges during the inter-war years for expressing opposition to fascism. I wasn't aware of these connections when I first became interested in Montale. Who knows what subconscious influences draw us toward a piece of literature?

The versions in this pamphlet were selected from Eugenio Montale's five collections, originally published over a fifty-year period. When deciding which pieces to work with I chose poems that appealed most to me and those I felt I could do justice to. However, it often seemed as if the poems were choosing me. If translation of poetry is about staying alert to the possibilities of meaning, it sometimes felt as if these possibilities were infinite. Perhaps the hardest aspect of working on these versions was to stop working on them. My main aim was to achieve a balance between fidelity to the essence of the original and fidelity to my own voice.

Many critics consider Montale's early work to be eclipsed by later, more sophisticated poems. I was originally drawn to the short poems in his first collection. Their style has been described as 'nihilistic modernism', but I feel that the metaphysical emptiness to be found in them is not only experienced and recognised but also embraced.

Montale's work does not have 'designs' upon us; it does not attempt to impose ideology or coerce the reader into a point of view. Instead, Montale's journey from the post-war wilderness leads us away from ideological and theological certainties. The middle period poems are infused with a sense of dread at the totalitarianism of the era and the approach of war. Profoundly political, their elliptical nature is only partly a result of a need for Montale to evade censorship. The poet's stated aim during this period was to write work that would "contain its own motives without revealing them or rather, without blurting them out." The late poems are another departure, utilising deadpan humour and a certain world weariness.

Existential questions in the face of political upheaval feel particularly relevant to the present. Montale's work has often been characterised as pessimistic, but his resigned observations of human imprudence and the resultant suffering seem to me to offer something close to solace. There is a sense that we have been here before.

DON'T ASK

Don't ask me to place a frame round
the human condition, to trace the soul's
shapeless form, for a poem that will blaze
like a crocus on a drought-struck lawn.

Imagine the man of action, composed,
self-assured, a friend to himself and others;
does he care if the sun prints his shadow
on a derelict wall?

Don't ask me for formulas to encompass
worlds. I only have these syllables, gnarled
as branches. All I can tell you here and now
is what we are not, what we don't want.

MIDDAY

Lie in shade, lost in thought
beside the sun trap of a garden wall.
Hear the blackbird's alarm
when an adder rustles the thorn.

Watch red ants file out of cracks
in the earth, pouring over scrub
and vetch, tiny chains that break
and re-link across the tips of leaves.

Listen through palm fronds
to the distant crash of the sea,
the shrill of cicadas on the bare
slopes of the valley.

Go out into the midday sun,
downcast and stunned to feel
life's nothing but a walk beside
a wall topped with broken bottles.

LIGHT

Why head for the shadow
of that stand of trees
like a kestrel dropping out of summer's heat?

Leave the soporific reeds
in their bed, come instead
and watch life on its journey

toward dust. Walk out into
this haze, a glare that will
make you feel weak.

Those clouded mountain tops
are like us, hidden from ourselves
and from others.

The serenity of the sky depends
on only one certainty. Light.

SUNFLOWER

Bring me a sunflower to plant
in this garden parched by sea salt.
All day it's face will follow the sun.

From out of darkness bodies
are draw toward light. To merge
and blend is the fate of everything.

Bring me a sunflower to trace the sun's
trajectory while its essence escapes in haze;
bring me a sunflower, its face ablaze.

THE EVIDENCE

I've seen suffering
in a choked stream, brittle veins
on a parched leaf, in the eye
of a fallen horse.

But I've hardly ever seen
its opposite. Only evidence
of divine indifference; in the statues
of the soporific park, in a white cloud
and in the high-flying hawk.

SYRIA

The ancients wrote
that poetry brings you
closer to god. Maybe not
if you're reading mine.
But I knew it was true
the day my voice returned
through a wrap of cloud
as goats rattled from a crag
to cascade across
the road, settling to graze
on blackthorn burs
broom and sedge,
while sun and moon
melted and fused,
that day the engine died
and an arrow of blood on a stone
showed the way to Aleppo.

PORTOVENERE

The Tritone flows from waves
that lap the sill of a Christian temple,
and every new hour
is as old as the last.
Doubt is led away like a child
holding a parent's hand.

No one can stay
self-absorbed for long
among these foundations,
and it's foolish to decide
on anything while you're here;
later, when you leave,
you can assume a face to wear.

FROWN

I saw a crease on the brow
of the most impassive face;
pain, glimpsed for an instant,
gone in a crowded street.

Words can mimic the wind
blowing in the heart's hollows.
But deeper truths exist in silence
where a sob is a song of peace.

SMOKE

I'd wait for you at the station,
cough in the cold and fog,
buy a newspaper not worthy of that name,
smoke cigarettes that came
in those bright packets
before the law changed.

If your train was cancelled or late
I'd scan the carriages as they passed,
find your face on the platform,
nearly always last.
It's just one of the ways
you haunt me in dreams.

RAIN

When a downpour
broke the drought, little children
danced naked on the shore.

The traveller sat behind glass
remembering when clothes
and even names were superfluous.

WIND AND FLAGS

I remember how the wind
that carries a taste of sea into the valley
wrapped her dress around her body
and tangled her hair against the sky.

Today, its unfaltering breath
passes through this garden,
rocking the empty hammock
where she drifted in a dream.

Time never moulds a sand dune
the same way twice. If it did,
our love story and this version of life
would cease to exist.

And this is what sets us free.
But my reverie isn't going anywhere.
Flags and bunting stir above the village
where a band is starting up.

The world is palpable after all,
and I'm surprised by this
stream of weary people
who gather in the square to dance.

SHOOT GROWING IN A WALL

Like the gnomon of a sundial
the shadow of this shoot,
rooted in brick and plaster,
tracks the sun's trajectory,
a shape lifted from a shape
the way smoke lifts from flame.

This morning the shoot
is shadow-less, glazed
in last night's rain. Looking out,
the sea is taking on light
and a trawler with three masts
slips from harbour. The deck gleams,
the rudder leaves no crease.

THE DEAD

A wave breaks, becomes a spume cloud
absorbed by sand flats.
This iron coast is where hope came,
more desperate than the sea,
where an azure plain
gives way to green.

        The north wind
smooths muddied currents, turns them back
to where they began.
Nets hang on branches by the path,
faded, drying in late light.
Above, the blue deepens, glinting with stars
as it arcs into a wave-lashed horizon.

        Kelp is dragged up
on the beach, but our lives refuse
such helpless indignity: the part of us
we thought had stopped, resigned to its limits,
somehow rages on, and the heart struggles
like a marsh hen, caught in the mesh
of one of those nets.

        Maybe the dead
aren't at rest either; maybe a force
more pitiless than life
pulls them back to these beaches.
Their shadows move across
our memories, silent, formless,
close enough to brush our skin,
to remind us of their existence
before they're lost in the sea's sieve.

THE WIND ON THE CRESCENT

Edinburgh

The Forth bridge didn't bring me to your door.
In those days, I would have navigated the sewers
to be with you. But my strength was waning
like the evening sun on those Georgian windows.

A street preacher on the Crescent asked me
"Do you know where to find God?"
I knew, and so I told him. He shook his head
and took off in a whirlwind that sent men and houses
spiralling up into the dark.

I'M NOT ASKING

for fixed geology, reliable faces,
material wealth. Lately, in this restless circle
bitter and sweet taste the same.

Even a heart now intent on no more
than steady time can be surprised,
like a flock of birds taking flight
after a rifle's report.

LEMON TREES

I hear some poet laureates
wander only in landscaped gardens
with borders full of Ligustrum,
acanthus and box. I prefer roads
that lead to muddy ditches
where a boy probing with a stick
might lift out a skinny eel;
paths that drop down
through reed beds, open
into lemon groves.

Even better if the birds aren't home,
dissolved somewhere in the blue
and nothing is louder
than the wind in the branches
and the scent of fruit rises
undiluted. The constant din
is hushed, political quarrel
out of earshot for a while.
Even the poor feel rich
where the air is scented by lemons.

In a near silence like this
it feels as if everything
has dropped its defences ;
that a secret is about to be revealed;
as if an unravelling thread
will lead to the still point
at the centre of reality, a link
that can't hold. You can feel
nature's symmetry, breathing citrus
as the day cools, almost believing
in a fading human shadow.

Now the city sky's dissected
and obscured by towers,
the air is a conduit for fumes and noise
and even the ground
is tired of the rain. It seems this winter
doesn't know when to stop.
But I remember an errand
to another part of town, a door
open to a courtyard, a glimpse of trees
with branches full of lemons,
each a bell, chiming with light.

DEATH DIDN'T TROUBLE YOU

    From *'Xenia II'*

Death didn't trouble you.
Even though your dogs had died,
and that psychiatrist known as Mad Uncle.
Even your mother with her speciality,
risotto and frog's legs, a Milanese 'triumph.'
And your father who's image appraised me
day and night from his shrine on the wall.
But death didn't trouble you at all.

It was me who attended funerals,
reclining in a taxi, keeping my distance
from tears, huddles of mourners.
Living didn't seem to bother you either;
displays of vanity, obscene appetites,
occasions when humans behave like wolves.

A tabula rasa then, except for one thing
and that was beyond me, but to you, it mattered.

THE SHOEHORN

For a long time, we mourned the rusty shoehorn.
It had travelled with us everywhere, a lewd intruder
in a world of stucco, linen, gold leaf.
It must have been at the *Danieli*
when I forgot to slide it into the suitcase,
and maybe Hedia, the chambermaid, lobbed it
into the Grand Canal. How could I ask them
to look for that battered slip of tin?
An image (ours) was at stake,
and Hedia, the dependable, had kept it safe.

YOU

You were always astute,
whether exiting the mouth of Etna
or the jaws of a glacier,
making connections, deductions.

Remember the good Dr Mangano,
how he smiled when you exposed him
as a blunt instrument of the fascists?

That was you all over; even on a precipice
sweetness and horror were in harmony.

HAWKS

Hawks
always out of range of your eyesight,
rarely close enough for you to see them.
There was one in Étretat, keeping vigil
over the awkward flights of his fledglings.
Two others in Greece on the via Delfi,
a scuffle of feathers and juvenile beaks,
brash and harmless.

You preferred life when it was being torn
apart, the rip of its insufferable
swaddling.

THE FLOOD

The flood swept up furniture and papers,
drowned paintings and pictures
that crammed an underground,
double-locked garage. Maybe they surged
together, books bound in red Moroccan leather,
Du Bo's verbose dedications, a wax seal
depicting Ezra's beard, Alain's take on *Valery*,
a manuscript of *Orphic Songs,*
shaving brushes, junk, keepsakes,
and all of your brother Silvio's compositions.
For ten, maybe twelve days,
they floated in an oily soup
before finally giving up their identity.
I'm grimed to the neck too, although
my civilised reputation was never entirely credible;
not mired in the aftermath of flood,
but in the events of an unbelievable,
and never believed, reality.
Strength to face this truth was the first thing
you lent me, and maybe you never knew.

RED ON RED

It's not spring yet
but already the heads of geraniums
appear above the sill.
Soon, the window will be filled
by foliage and frantic ants.
A ladybird traverses
my tax return, red on red.
Maybe she'll do me a favour
and fill it in. The church bell
rings, phones disturb the peace,
and the newsreader drones on
about fatalities on the motorway,
a record for an Easter Monday.

THE KINGFISHER

Some believe
the Kingfisher searches for nothing
but souls.

I've seen more than one
dash the surface of dull water
with a flash of lapis lazuli.

His kingdom is measured in millimetres,
his flight
by an arrow of light.

Only the Kingfisher
has his measurements correct;
others only have a soul
and the fear
of losing it.

THE BIG DEAL

What it was about nobody ever knew.
A rush of blood, act of rebellion
or the pure embodiment of thoughtlessness.
What was left was illegitimate
half and half, uncertain.

No one had wished these consequences
on them-self; only on others. This state
wasn't manmade, the declarations
of stray dogs, and the perfect
monsters growling here and there.

REMORSE

I feel remorse for having squashed
the mosquito on the wall, the ant
on the floor. I feel remorse but still I'm here,
dark suited for the conference, the reception.
I feel sorrow for everything, even the lacky
who offers me advice on investment,
remorse for the beggar to whom
I gave no change, grief for the insane man
who leads the administration.

HISTORY

doesn't unwind flexibly
like a chain. Even if it did,
chain links
don't always hold.
History doesn't contain
a before and after
and nothing in history
becomes more tender
after simmering
over a low flame.

History isn't made by
its students, nor by those
who would ignore it. It doesn't find
its own way. Being obstinate,
it hates gradual progress,
and neither advances
nor retreats, but switches tracks.
Its destination isn't timetabled.
History doesn't justify
or regret; it is not innate, being external.
History delivers neither caress
nor whiplash. It is not a teacher
of anything that concerns us
and recording it
doesn't make it true or fair.

History is not
an excavator, leaving tunnels,
crypts, hiding places. A few
survive history. It is benevolent,
generous in its destruction;
better of course

if it destroyed more, but history
can't keep up with developments
or avenge
every new vendetta.

History drags its net
on the bottom. It is ripped
in places, so some
slip away. If you meet an escapee
he won't be particularly happy,
being ignorant of his freedom,
having spoken to no-one. The others
left behind in the net
will believe they are freer than him.

GÖTTERDÄMMERUNG

I read that the twilight of the Gods
is about to begin. Whoever wrote that
was mistaken. Beginnings are always unrecognizable,
and any definition can be punctured with a pin.

Twilight began when man considered himself
more dignified than moles or crickets, and a recurring hell
is hardly a rehearsal for a grand premier, long postponed
because the director is ill, busy, or holed up somewhere,
and no one can replace him.

ACKNOWLEDGEMENTS

My thanks to my editor and publisher John Lucas and to Rachel for her continued support and belief. Thanks also to Rory Waterman, Richard Skinner and Martin Malone for their encouragement.

Special thanks to Caterina for her assistance with 'Il grande affare.'

I am grateful to the editors of *New Walk* and *The High Window* where versions of some of these poems have appeared. The poem 'Syria' was published in *The Great Animator*.

SELECTED BIBLIOGRAPHY

Eugenio Montale, *Ossi di Seppia,* Mondadori (Milan, 1948)

Selected poems, Ed. by G. Singh, Manchester University Press (Manchester, 1975)

Jonathan Galassi, *Eugenio Montale, Collected Poems 1929-1954,* Bilingual Edition, Farrar, Straus and Giroux, (New York, 2012)

William Arrowsmith, *The Collected Poems of Eugenio Montale, 1925–1977,* Norton, (New York, 2012)

Mario Petrucci, *Xenia,* Arc Publications, (Todmorden, 2016)